Crossing 13

Memoir of a Father's Suicide

Carrie Stark Hugus

To Susie with
blessings.

Carrie Hugus

What Others Are Saying About This Book

Carrie Stark Hugus has written a book, Crossing 13: Memoir of a Father's Suicide, *that will help many people heal from the pain of losing someone through suicide. The reader grows through hearing Carrie's very personal story, and is offered resources and direction on how to proceed.*

Gerald Jampolsky, M.D. Coauthor of *Mini Course for Life* and *Finding Our Way Home*, and recipient of the Pride in the Profession Award given by the American Medical Association

Few authors can approach the most difficult subjects in a manner where the reader not only receives solutions, but also feels deeply understood and validated. In Crossing 13: Memoir of a Father's Suicide, *Carrie Stark Hugus accomplishes this through sharing her deeply personal journey. This book shall touch all who read it, and for those who have suffered the loss of a loved one through suicide, it offers immediate help, hope, and new direction.*

Dr. Lee Jampolsky, best-selling author of *Healing the Addictive Personality* and *Smile for No Good Reason*

Heartbreaking and bleakly honest, Carrie shares her struggle to find a new normal following the suicide of her father just as she enters her teens. Young survivors of a parent's suicide will identify with and benefit from recognizing that their confusing, frightening grief responses are normal for what they have experienced. They will be encouraged by learning Carrie has grown through her grief and now enjoys a happy, stable adulthood.

LaRita Archibald, Founder of HEARTBEAT Support for Survivors after Suicide

Powerful and brings to light an often overlooked group of survivors. Kudos to Carrie for her willingness to share her story!

Jarrod Hindman, Program Manager, Office of Suicide Prevention, Prevention Services Division, Colorado Department of Public Health and Environment

This courageous account of one little girl's journey to understand why shows us that suicide changes everyone it touches and it takes a lifetime to recover. Crossing 13 will open your eyes, break your heart and touch your soul.

Tamra Monahan, author,
Colorado's Best Bed and Breakfasts

Through Carrie's authentic and courageous story of living through her father's suicide, we learn how to move beyond the depths of despair to a life of peace, profound empathy, wisdom, joy, and self-love. This book is masterful in healing any person who has experienced great loss.

Karen Storsteen, M.S., Psychotherapist,
Grief Counselor, and Intuitive

Grateful acknowledgment is made for permission to print
"Reinforcement in the Aftermath of Suicide" by LaRita Archibald.

First Edition 2008

ISBN 978-0-9815938-0-7

Library of Congress Control Number 2008901380

Affirm Publications, LLC
www.affirmpublications.com

This book is dedicated to my mother and sisters.
And for my father,

Cameron John Stark, Jr.

December 25, 1940—October 13, 1979

Preface

Approximately 24,000 children, aged 18 and under[1] suffer from the death of a parent to suicide each year in the United States. Based on this estimate, there are 700,000 children who became survivors of suicide in the last 29 years. Of this group, 80%[2] grieve for their father. I am among their company . . . a teen survivor.

One of the largest numbers of suicide deaths is among men, between 24 and 44[3] years of age. My father is part of this group . . . he was 38 years old when he died.

This book is a personal account of my life, written from my memories of myself as a thirteen-year-old whose life changed suddenly and dramatically during and after the death of my father.

Although this is an accurate description of events from my perspective, some names have been changed

---

[1] Estimated figure based on the average number of children expected by men (2.2), and median age man father's his first child (25.1 years) from the United States Department of Health and Human Services National Vital Statistic Report Source: Series 23, No. 26, Table 12.

[2] Suicide Prevention Action Network, Quick Facts about Suicide.

[3] United States Department of Health and Human Services Preliminary Deaths 2005 Report, Table 7.

to respect the privacy of those described through the eyes of that thirteen-year-old girl.

It is my intention through this personal story to break down societal stigmas related to suicide and its survivors. My hope is to create sensitivity awareness, especially for child survivors, to bring about change through open dialog.

Contents

Foreword

Reinforcement in the Aftermath of Suicide

RESPONSIBILITY: Putting it into perspective.

I have a responsibility TO those I love . . .
to be loving, patient, considerate and kind,
to be loyal, respectful and honest,
to be appreciative, encouraging and comforting,
to share myself and care for myself;

. . . to be the best possible "ME" . . .

BUT

I am not responsible FOR them . . .
not for their achievements, successes or triumphs,
not for their joy, gratification or fulfillment,

not for their defeats, failures or disappointments,
not for their thoughts, choices or mistakes,

. . . And, most of all, not for their suicide . . .

For HAD I been responsible,
this death would not have occurred.

—LaRita Archibald, Founder
HEARTBEAT*

---

* HEARTBEAT is peer support group offering empathy, encouragement, and direction following the suicide of a loved one. For more information visit www.heartbeatsurvivorsaftersuicide.org.

My Story

Reflecting

When we lose a loved one to disease or an accident, it is easier to retain happy memories of them. We know that, if they could choose, they would still be here with us. But it's not as easy for the suicide survivor. Because our loved one seems to have made a choice that is abhorrent to us, we feel disconnected and "divorced" from their memory. We are in a state of conflict with them, and we are left to resolve that conflict alone.

—Jeffrey Jackson, American Association of Suicidology,
Handbook for Suicide Survivors

October 13, 1979: 9:00 p.m.

"Good night," Mom says with a kiss, weepy eyes, and an attempt at a reassuring smile. As she shuts the door to my room, a feeling of guilt-ridden nausea flutters about in my stomach. I lie alone in the dark, struggling to absorb the lingering images of the day. Shock has overtaken sorrow, keeping the tears corked tightly inside. "I'm still the same person," I reassure myself. Up until several hours ago, I had lived a fairly sheltered life and I thought my family was just like any other family.

We are—or were—family of five including a mother, three daughters, and a father. These things only happen in crazy families, not normal families like ours. What will people think of us now? How could I be so blindsided? Am I dreaming or did the events of today really happen?

I hear the coyotes howling outside as I lie in the darkness of my bedroom. This familiar sound takes me back to what I thought was my reality, my life as I knew it before today. I struggle for answers and clues leading up to this morning's tragedy, trying to find meaning in my father's acts.

I will just take it one step at a time, I reassure myself. Then, as if it is I who is walking though the doorway of death, instead of my father, my life begins to flash before my eyes.

Tracie

My sister, Tracie, just started first grade and will turn seven next week. She ties her straight, dirty-blond hair in two pigtails and her crooked front teeth sit perfectly between pudgy cheeks when she smiles.

She is a pretty cute kid, even though she likes playing in the dirt with Jonathan, the little boy next door. Mom once found Tracie and Jonathan sitting in a giant ant pile, building sand castles. Those crazy little kids didn't even feel the army ants crawling all over them, let alone the bites, until the welts started rising an hour later.

Tracie has a stuffed toy Big Bird that she clutches tightly by its bright orange foot. That gives her the leverage she needs to swing it over her head so she can gouge people with its sharp plastic beak when she's angry with them.

Tracie loves cats, especially our barn cat Brandy. Brandy is a feisty cat who would scratch your eyes out for no reason. My little sister is the only one who can get close to that darn cat. Tracie's favorite game is to dress Brandy in doll clothes and push her around for hours in a shoebox. It is amazing to watch that mean old cat sit calmly in the box with her ears turned down while this little kid pushes her all around the house as if she's racing in the Indy 500. Tracie has done this for as long as I can remember and has yet to get bitten or scratched.

Each night Tracie brings her blanket and pillow into my room and makes her bed underneath my yellow desk. I think she likes lying next to the warmth of the heat register. One night Brandy came into my room chasing a mouse and they both ran right over her. Tracie awoke screaming and crying. She nearly scared me to death.

Tracie is always crying. When she was a baby, she fell down the stairs, bit her tongue, and had to get stitches. Mom sat me down and told me that I had to be careful not to make Tracie cry so her tongue could heal. I kept thinking that Mom was expecting the impossible because nothing could stop my little sister from crying and you could never figure out what would set her off in the first place.

I had become accustomed to tuning out my sisters cries. One day I was sitting in front of the television and masterfully blocked out the sounds of Tracie falling down the stairs, less than twenty feet away. I even managed to ignore her screaming and crying as she lay at the bottom of the stairs, covered in cereal and milk. Mom was very angry and asked me why I didn't help. She couldn't believe it when I told her I hadn't heard a thing.

Tammy

I'm afraid of my big sister, Tammy. She is a skinny, freckled, redhead with a mean streak. She thinks she's cool because she's seventeen.

Tammy says we are opposites. She calls me her little jock sister because I play sports. She calls herself a freak. I'm not sure what freaks are exactly, except that they wear tight, torn blue jeans with peace signs on the rear end. I'm pretty sure my sister smokes cigarettes and I have seen her sneak out of the house, late at night, more than once.

But that was before she left. A few months ago, Tammy ran away from home. She dropped out of school to live with her boyfriend, Jim. I don't understand why she left school because she only had two months to go until graduation. I know this made Mom and Dad mad, but I'm happy she's gone.

When Tammy was still at home, she and Mom argued a lot. Sometimes during dinner, Tammy made her so mad that Mom would get up from the table and chase after her. Tracie and I just sat quietly, afraid to move an inch. I wasn't sure what Mom would have done if she had ever caught Tammy; I only hoped I wasn't going to be around to see it.

Tammy likes to bully me. Before she left, she locked me out of our house in my underwear on several occasions. Tammy especially enjoyed this game when it was snowing. She and Tracie laughed at me from the kitchen window as I stood freezing in the front yard. She has also done things like make me eat dog food and tickle me until I wet my pants. Yet, even though her favorite entertainment is to make me suffer, she won't let anyone else pick on me. It's a strange relationship, and I don't pretend to understand it.

I think Tammy tries to be so tough because she almost died twice. The first time her appendix exploded and Mom had to rush her to the hospital in the middle of the night. The second time, she fell off her horse, Bars. She was running him on a dirt road and when she turned onto the paved road, Bars lost his footing and rolled with Tammy on him. She ended up unconscious in a ditch. The ambulance came and she was in the hospital for over a week. When I went to visit her, she had a black eye as big as the one Rocky Balboa had in the movie, *Rocky*.

After Tammy moved out, I promptly moved into her bedroom in the basement. This room is bigger than my old room and I have my very own bathroom. Best of all, I'm farther away from Tracie and her Big Bird.

Mom

Mom takes care of us, keeps our house spotless and has dinner on the table at 6:00 p.m. each night. Mom is very particular about the bathrooms and our green shag carpet. When guests are coming, the first thing we do is clean the bathrooms. Then she brings out the heavy Kirby vacuum and attaches this funny looking red rake to the front. It's oddly fun to watch Mom use that red rake to pull up the matted down multigreen fibers.

Once a month my parents have a poker party. Tracie and I love these occasions because the next morning we get down on our hands and knees under the dining room table and look for pennies buried in the shag carpet. We love this treasure hunt each Sunday because there is nothing on TV except church programs. I have often wondered if God would get angry if one of the networks ran cartoons instead.

Mom recently graduated from beauty school. During her nine months of study, Mom turned our basement laundry room into a salon. In her makeshift salon, she kept manikin heads with long hair to practice cutting hair, rolling permanents, and applying color. Once she had mastered manikin heads, she moved on to practicing on my sister and me.

As I sat in front of the clothes dryer, staring at the cement walls, Mom attempted to cut my hair so it would flip out and feather back on the sides, which was exactly how I wanted it to look. She then moved on to my eyebrows, using hot wax to separate my thick unibrow into two smaller shapelier brows. It was fun playing beauty shop with Mom, even though it was sometimes difficult to sit still on the hard stool for what seemed like hours.

Once Mom graduated, she immediately went to work full time at a salon about thirty minutes from our house. I am still getting used to the fact that she is working. She isn't there to meet me when I come home from school and she isn't around on Saturday anymore.

Grandma

Grandma Stark, Dad's mom, moved in with us a few years ago, after Grandpa Stark died. Dad built her an entire apartment at the end of our house, complete with two bedrooms and a kitchen. Our house looked odd after Grandma's apartment was attached. Her apartment was built on the opposite side of the garage, adding length to the rectangular structure. Right smack in the middle, connecting these two rectangular buildings, is the garage, which has become the focal point of our house—and, now, my life.

When I was younger, and before we moved to this house, we lived down the street from Grandma and Grandpa. They had a wonderful garden full of strawberries, grape vines, miniature statues, and a goldfish pond. My favorite statue was one of a little boy fishing at the pond. I always felt like *Alice in Wonderland* when I wandered through their elaborate garden.

Each fall Grandma canned vegetables and made rhubarb pies. Grandpa made his famous horseradish sauce. One night at dinner Grandpa tested his new batch of horseradish sauce. After the first bite, his eyes started to water and tears streamed down his face. He got a huge smile on his face and proudly stated it was the best batch he'd ever made. I thought it was strange to prepare and eat something that makes you cry.

Tracie enjoys hanging out with Grandma. She will spend the entire day in Grandma's apartment playing cards. Sometimes Grandma wanders around our house at night and has trouble finding her way back to her apartment. I overheard Dad tell Mom that she has hardening of the arteries, which is why she forgets things. I told this to my friend, Cindy, one day while playing Barbie dolls under our deck. That night Dad and Mom told me I was not to repeat that anymore. Dad's eyes had tears in them as he scolded me about Grandma.

A feeling of uneasiness washed over me when I saw sadness in my strong father's eyes. The only other time I had seen Dad upset was after Grandpa died.

Before Grandpa died, we visited him in the hospital every night. Kids were not allowed in the room, so Tammy and I had to stay in the waiting area for what seemed like hours. Mom and Dad would buy us waxed lips that you could chew on and they tasted like cherries. One night Dad came down to check on us and saw me running around the waiting area. He promptly grabbed me by my arm and took me out to the car for a spanking. My father had never hit me before and when the spanking was over, he hugged me and cried.

Dad

Dad is a traveling salesman. When I was younger, I liked it when he went out of town because I could sleep with Mom while he was gone and when Dad returned, he would give me a gift from his travels.

Dad likes playing practical jokes. During my first trip to California, I noticed there were white bumps on the roads as lane dividers instead of white lines. I asked Dad why traffic lanes had bumps and he said with a grin, "That way blind people can drive." I had to ponder that one for a while. He also tried to convince me that chocolate milk came from brown cows, but I did not buy that one.

One time, during a sleepover with my friends, he listened in while we played "light as a feather, stiff as a board." In that game, one person lies down on the ground while the others put two fingers under their body. As we conjure up the spirits, asking for help to lift the person magically into the air, we repeat in unison, "Light as a feather, stiff as a board." During the ceremony that particular night, we asked for a sign from the spirits to let us know when it was time to lift the body. At that moment, Dad turned off the house lights from the breaker box. As screams penetrated the house, I heard dad's faint laughter coming from the backyard.

Sunday is our family day. Dad is usually home and I wake to the smell of chili and cheese omelets, Dad's specialty. Then Mom packs a picnic lunch and we head to the mountains to find a perfect spot by the river and spend the day playing in the sun, eating fried chicken and potato salad.

People are always comparing Dad to the actor Burt Reynolds. I guess it's because he has dark hair and a mustache. Once he shaved off his mustache and Tracie wouldn't go near him for a week because she had never seen him without it and didn't recognize her own father.

My favorite place in the whole wide world is Dad's lap. I feel so calm and safe when I curl up next to him and place my head on his lap. His hand automatically rests on my scalp as his fingers play with my hair. I cherish this intimate time and take advantage of it whenever I can, whether it's driving in the car or watching television.

Carrie

I often play in the dry creek bed behind our house, climb trees, and catch salamanders. I also like to ride my silvery-gray mare, Angel, through the alfalfa fields that surround our house, accompanied by my dogs, Oliver and Daisy. At night I hear the harmony of the crickets competing with the howling of the coyotes. Although our dogs are free to roam during the day, they come in at night. Sometimes I hear Oliver howling at the coyotes, as if talking to them. As I listen, I secretly wish I could understand their conversation.

Each morning, I walk to the barn to feed Tammy's copper horse, Bars, a flake of hay and a scoop of grain. Then I feed Angel the exact same meal. I am always leery when reaching into the grain barrel because it is a magnet for field mice. It doesn't matter how many times I come across a field mouse; it always startles me. But worse than encountering field mice is the chore of cleaning the stalls. It takes most of Saturday morning to accomplish this task. First I lift the heavy piles of manure with large shovels and dump them into the big red wheel barrel. Then Tammy and I struggle to roll the wheel barrel to the end of the corral and dump its contents down the steep hill, where they come to rest in the ditch.

After my chores, I like to meet up with Cindy and Anne to race our bikes around the circular dirt road that connects the dozen or so homes in our neighborhood. Near Halloween, Anne, Cindy, and I spend hours turning Anne's basement into a haunted house that scares the living daylights out of the neighborhood kids and our parents. The best year was when we turned the vacuum cleaner into a ghost. We took a doll and put fake blood on it and as soon as our victims passed the bloody baby in her crib, we turned on the vacuum and the ghost floated up in the air. I was most pleased when Mom screamed and put her hands on her chest to catch her breath. At the end of the tour Mom hugged me, laughed, and said it was the best haunted house ever.

Three weeks ago I started seventh grade. Middle school is a lot different than elementary school. Boys are now shorter than I am and I worry that I'm not as well liked as I was last year. Sixth grade was much easier. I had one class of twenty kids to get along with. Now I have five different classes with twenty kids in each class to get along with.

The principal at my new school doesn't like me. My first day, she called me into her office and sternly said that she knew I was Tammy's sister and that she would not put up with any misbehavior. As I sat in the chair in front of her enormous desk, I felt my chest and face turning red and felt resentment toward my freaky sister.

I learned quickly that to survive in middle school, I must blend in with the crowd and be exactly like the other kids. Everyone who is anyone wears the same clothes—the uniform of Levi's button-down jeans, an Izod shirt, and Adidas shoes. I begged Mom to buy me Adidas but she said it was ridiculous to spend $35 on a pair of shoes. I lucked out when Mom's brother came to visit from California and found a 50-percent-off sale on Adidas in the paper. Uncle Fred drove me to the other side of town so I could buy my Adidas with the money I'd earned babysitting the kids next door.

October 13, 1979: 10:00 p.m.

As I continue to think about my life, I know that things will never be the same. Yesterday, I was a normal girl who loved adventure and looked forward to exploring life as a teenager. And now, less than twelve hours later, I am the daughter of a widow.

My father left no note explaining why he did what he did, leaving me consumed with questions and regrets. What could I have done to prevent this? Why didn't I see this coming? Why didn't I have the courage to enter the garage and try to stop him sooner? How could everything I grew up thinking and believing about my father be a lie?

I don't know this man who killed himself. I am afraid that people will think he was crazy, weird, and weak, which doesn't describe my dad. My dad was a large, strong man who loved to make us laugh. He was not crazy and wouldn't leave me. My dad didn't drink, beat us, or do mean things. I wanted to defend my father and shout to the world that he was not crazy, that he took good care of us, and that he loved us and would never hurt us.

Suddenly the stark reality of the day creeps over me like a harsh, cold frost: Dad was a stranger. This morning he became a crazy person who didn't love us and left us forever. He hurt us and inflicted a wound on me that may never heal.

As I lie in my bed listening to the sounds of Mom's tears echoing through the heating ducts above, I am terrified to let my weary body drift off to sleep. What if I keep reliving the events of this awful day over and over again in my dreams? The horror of what I was exposed to replays in my mind.

I ask myself, "Will these images haunt me for the rest of my life?"

"No," I fiercely promise myself. I make a vow to myself that this will not break me. "I will grow up to live a normal life," I whisper confidently to comfort myself.

As the fatigue of the day takes over, I begin to fall asleep repeating these words over and over:

"I will not become a crazy person, I will not become a crazy person, I will not become a crazy person, I will not become . . . my father."

Signs?

Many survivors struggle to understand the reasons for the suicide, asking themselves over and over again: "Why?" Many replay their loved ones' last days, searching for clues, particularly if they didn't see any signs that suicide was imminent.

—American Foundation for Suicide Prevention

Summer 1979

After dinner on Sundays, my father and I retreated to the basement to watch TV. Most nights we watched the *Muppet Show* or the *Wonderful World of Disney*. When these shows weren't on, we searched for a movie and then escaped together into the story plot.

One Sunday we watched a movie about a teenaged boy who was very unhappy. He didn't think his friends really liked him and his father frequently picked on him and put him down. One night the boy went into his father's office, sat down at his desk, pulled out a piece of paper from the desk drawer, and wrote a note. He then went over to his father's gun cabinet and pulled out a gun. He found a box of bullets in the drawer of the gun cabinet and then loaded the gun, one bullet at a time. Then he took the gun, put it to his head, and . . . bang! The show cut to commercial. I sat up, troubled by what I had just seen, and looked at Dad.

"What happened?" I asked.

"He committed suicide."

"What's suicide?" I asked.

"Suicide is when a person takes his own life."

"Do you know anybody who has killed himself?" I asked, concerned.

"No."

"Why did that boy kill himself?"

"Because he was very unhappy."

This was very disturbing to me. Dad had always been a man of few words, but I couldn't believe he was so unemotional about this. Maybe it was because he was an adult and already knew all about such things, so it no longer bothered him, but still . . . Then a thought came to me.

"Dad?" I nervously asked.

"Yes," he replied, looking straight into my eyes.

"Would you ever commit suicide?"

He looked at me for what seemed to be an eternity and then a warm smile formed on his face.

"No, it's just a movie. It's not real," he said.

He put his large, warm hand on my shoulder and pulled me toward him. I felt relieved. Once we released one another from our hug, I repositioned myself on the couch, with my head in his lap, to watch the rest of the movie.

I began having recurring dreams about dying after that Sunday movie. At first I had dreams about the boy

I saw in the movie. Then the boy turned into Dad. I dreamt that Dad was driving our red Pacer and was hit by another driver. In the dream, Dad would get into the car, drive up the steep dirt road leading out of our neighborhood, and pull out onto the main road to town. A large truck would come barreling down the road and hit the Pacer on the driver's side. I always awoke frightened and disoriented.

I also had dreams that Dad died of cancer, like my grandfather. In those dreams, Mom and I held hands as we entered the hospital. Dad lay in bed with tubes coming out of his arms and the machines to which he was connected were noisy. I would awaken when the machine next to his head stopped beeping and a straight line appeared on the screen.

I never told Mom or Dad about these recurring dreams because I knew they would think I was watching too much television and that Mom wouldn't let me see movies with Dad on Sundays anymore.

One Saturday afternoon I played with my Barbie doll in my bedroom, spending most of the morning creating a house for her. I unfolded and stood my tri-fold albums on end for the walls, made a Kleenex box into a sofa, and used my Easy Bake Oven for the stove. As I admired my hard work, I felt a presence behind me and turned to see Dad standing in the doorway.

"Hi Daddy," I said. "Look what I made?"

"That's nice honey," he said, with sadness in his voice.

"There's something I want to tell you," he added as he sat down on the bed, patting his hand on the spot next to him for me to sit down.

I crawled up on my bed and Dad grabbed hold of me and began sobbing on my shoulder. I felt my shirt become damp from his tears and all I could think of was how to get away from him. I had never really seen my father cry like this before. It was uncommon in my family for either of my parents to show such emotion. I wasn't sure what to do. I didn't know how to comfort an adult.

"Your mother has asked me to move out," he managed to get out through the tears.

I was startled and alarmed. I could not grasp what he was saying.

"We're getting a divorce," he said, looking at me as tears streamed from his bloodshot eyes.

I just sat, stunned and expressionless, staring back at my father, trying to comprehend what he was saying. I wondered where my mother was and why she wasn't with Dad as he gave me this frightening and confusing news.

Dad told me he didn't know why Mom didn't want to be married to him any more, said he was very sad, and admitted he was going to miss me very much. He said he didn't know how to tell Grandma and had no idea where he would live. He looked like a sad little boy to me and we sat together in silence for a long time.

I tried to think of something to say that would comfort him, but there was nothing that could break through the fog of my confusion.

Dad looked at me and asked, "Are you all right?"

"Yes," I replied, even though I wasn't. I felt anxious and I desperately wanted him to leave.

"Good," he said as he gave me a quick hug. Then he disappeared.

That night Mom was sitting in her green chair reading. This was always a good time to approach her to discuss things because she was relaxed and finished with her work for the day. We had a history of great conversations as she sat on her green chair and I perched on its matching stool. Sometimes she told me stories about her childhood. At other times we discussed and solved problems I was having. Sometimes she just listened to my ideas and dreams. Mom was always the person I went to for the answers to life's problems and mysteries. She had a talent for explaining things in a way I could understand and a gift for easing my troubled mind.

I had sought a great deal of Mom's counsel over the past year because strange things were happening to my body. I was the only girl in my sixth-grade class who had her period and wore a bra.

Mom helped me make arrangements with the school nurse for her to keep my tampons and allow me to use her bathroom during my time of the month. Mom also helped me buy bras that were not so noticeable under my clothes. By the end of the school year, I had become tall, gangly, and awkward. I hated gym because I had developed a tendency to trip and fall, which made the other kids laugh and call me Thud. Mom not only listened to my struggles in school, she also confided that the same thing happened to her when she was a girl. She promised that I would soon grow out of this awkward stage.

I crept up the stairs, carefully sat down on the footstool directly in front of my mother, and prepared myself for another reassuring conversation. She put down the paper and waited for me to say something.

"Mom . . ." I paused, gathering my courage to ask the question. "Are you and Dad getting a divorce?" I asked with concern.

Mom's body became stiff and her face became stern and cold.

"Why would you ask that?" she asked curtly.

Uh oh, I thought. I had seen this expression and heard that tone from my mother before and it wasn't good. My eyes darted back and forth as I tried to find a way out. I wasn't sure what to say. This was not the response I was looking for. I wanted Mom to hold me and say, "No, honey," in her soft, comforting voice, and then rock me like she did when I was little.

"Where did you hear that?" Mom asked brusquely.

"Dad told me today you were leaving him. Is this true?" I asked shyly, having managed the courage to answer her.

My mother looked very cross.

"What in the hell is he thinking? I can't believe that man would say something to you," she blurted out, shaking her head from side to side.

Then she looked directly at me with penetrating eyes and hissed, "No, I am not leaving your father. And don't you go repeating any of this to your sisters. You hear me!"

I nodded in reply.

"If I was leaving your Father, you would hear it from me. Do you understand?" She was almost yelling now.

I nodded again. With a loud sigh of frustration, Mom ordered me to bed. I quickly scurried off to my room before she could say anything else.

I was hurt and confused. Endless questions filled my mind. Why won't anyone think about me? Why didn't Mom give me a chance to tell her how strange Dad was today? Why couldn't Mom see that I was alone, scared, and needed to hear that everything would be all right? Why is Dad so sad and why is Mom so angry? All I wanted was someone to explain what was going on.

Celebrating 13

Most suicides are occasioned by a "catalyst" event: the breakup of a relationship, losing a job, or learning of bad news. Misconceptions arise when we mistake one of these isolated events for the cause of the suicide. Instead, it is more likely just the "straw that broke the camel's back."

—Jeffrey Jackson, American Association of Suicidology, *Handbook for Suicide Survivors*

October 8, 1979

Birthdays had always been a big deal in my family. As far back as I could remember I'd had special birthday parties.

When I was younger, Mom dressed me in a beautiful pink or yellow lace dress with ribbons in my hair and set a long table, fit for a queen, with a designated spot at the head for me. The neighborhood kids were invited for an afternoon of games, cake, and ice cream. Midway through the celebration, a clown or magician would arrive to entertain my guests and me. We would start planning my birthday a few weeks in advance and I could pick whatever I wanted to do.

For my thirteenth birthday, I asked Mom if I could go to dinner with just her and Dad. Mom arranged for a babysitter to look after Tracie. The night of my birthday, my parents and I dressed up for my night out on the town and went to an exotic restaurant where we had to take off our shoes and sit on the floor to eat. A dancer came by our table, draping Dad with her veils and shaking her navel rapidly to the beat of the music. I could tell this made Dad uncomfortable, but he was a good sport and watched politely until the dance was done.

I couldn't remember the last time I'd had Mom and Dad all to myself. I loved having their undivided attention, especially since things had been so strange in our house for several weeks. Dad had not been around much and Mom and I hadn't really had a green-chair talk since that puzzling night when I asked if she and Dad were getting a divorce.

I sneaked into my parent's room each day to inventory my father's clothes, just to make sure he hadn't moved out. There had been no further discussion about divorce between me and either of my parents, nor had there been any mention of the discussions we'd had on that bewildering day. I hadn't told my sisters or friends about those confusing conversations either.

The night of my birthday, our dinner seemed awkward at first and the conversation was forced. But Dad and Mom relaxed after a while and it felt like they were back to normal. Dad teased Mom and me. I laughed so hard I thought my food might come back up.

After dinner Mom asked, "What do you want to do next?"

"Let's go to Lookout Mountain to see the city lights from up high," I suggested, wanting to prolong the solo time with my parents as long as I could. As we drove up the winding narrow road, an idea came to me.

"Mom?" I called from the back seat of the car.

"Yes," she replied, in a warm and loving way.

"Didn't you and Dad grow up near here?"

"Yes."

"Will you tell me how you two met?" I asked.

"You know how we met," she replied.

"I know, but I want to hear the story again," I encouraged.

"All right," she sighed. "Your father and I met on a blind date," she began.

"Your Mom thought I was charming," Dad interjected with a chuckle, which made Mom chuckle too.

"That's not quite how it went," Mom replied good-naturedly. "I wasn't that impressed with your Father when we first met," she said smiling at my father.

My mother and father bantered with one another as Mom told the story of their courtship and I felt brilliant to have brought up the subject.

We arrived at the mountaintop and Dad parked the car. The thousands of tiny lights twinkling down in the city below us were a beautiful sight against the backdrop of the evening sky. It was a cold autumn night, so we stayed in the car and enjoyed the view as Mom continued her story.

As she talked, I pictured her as a teenager wearing a ponytail and poodle skirt, my father in black leather with greased-back hair. It always made me giggle to think of Mom and Dad dressed up like the characters on the TV show *Happy Days*.

Mom continued her story, adding that Dad had entered the army when he was seventeen and she was still in high school. He'd written to her from boot camp. They had gotten married when Mom was eighteen and were stationed in Gary, Indiana; then Tammy was born. Mom explained that they had been so poor that she would mix a box of corn flakes with their ration of hamburger to make it last throughout the month. Dad nodded in response and laughed at the memory.

I had seen old pictures of my parents when Tammy was a baby and found it strange to see them so young. My father had messy black hair and wore a white T-shirt with rolled up sleeves and blue Jeans. My mother looked like a little girl playing house, cradling my doll-sized sister, Tammy, in her arms.

After some urging from me in the back seat, I convinced my parents to again show me the houses they lived in while growing up. We drove back down the mountain and they gave me the tour. Afterward, they took me to park where they hung out when they were teenagers.

"Was this your make-out point?" I asked, teasing Mom.

"How do you know what make-out point is?" asked Mom, laughing.

"From TV," I explained. "Did you and Dad park here when you were dating?" I teased.

"That's none of your business," Mom said playfully.

I had been filled with joy as I watched my parents having fun sharing the intimate details of their past, and I'd felt completely happy and confident that I had succeeded in carrying out my secret mission of bringing my parents closer together.

As we started home I kept thinking what a wonderful night it had been and then a revelation came to me: maybe birthday wishes really did come true.

Knowing

The American Psychiatric Association ranks the trauma of losing a loved one to suicide as "catastrophic"—on par with that of a concentration camp experience.

October 13, 1979: Morning

It was a cool, sunny, autumn Saturday. The large cottonwood trees had turned golden and the sky was filled with cotton-ball clouds. I awoke to the magpies greeting me with their friendly good-morning song, got up, and went to the kitchen to pour myself a bowl of cereal. As I poured milk on my Frosted Flakes, Tracie burst through the kitchen, yelled a good-bye, and dashed out the front door. She was already dressed in jeans, T-shirt, and sneakers, clearly ready to take on the day. But the loud sound from the slamming door made me jump and spill my milk.

Mom had left a few hours earlier for work. I had a job babysitting the two little girls who lived next door to me. I liked babysitting for the Joy family because they seemed to be part of the hippy generation and I thought they were cool. They had long hair that was sometimes braided, tie-dyed shirts, and leather pants. The two little girls, Natalie and Kayla, slept in water-beds. I had never seen a real waterbed before, let alone a waterbed crib. Natalie was the older sister and had recently moved out of the crib into her own waterbed. I loved to take naps with her on that bed. It felt like being rocked by warm waves.

After breakfast, I got ready for my babysitting job. As I started to head downstairs to my bedroom, I heard a noise coming from the garage. I opened the door and saw my father standing by his workbench.

"Hi Daddy," I said in greeting.

He slowly turned around and said, "Hi."

"What are you doing?" I asked.

"When do you leave for babysitting?" he replied, answering my question with a question of his own.

"In half an hour," I replied.

"I want you to take your sister with you," he said.

"Why?" I whined, trying to avoid fulfilling his request.

"I have some work to do this morning and I don't want to be disturbed," he replied, rather coldly.

An uncomfortable feeling came over me. Neither his body language nor his tone was familiar to me. He was slumped over his bench, working, and he looked defeated and lifeless. His voice sounded distant and fatigued. Somehow, this didn't seem like my father.

"You better get going," he said with his back to me, as he continued working away.

I hesitated, then left and went to my room. I quickly changed my clothes and dragged a hairbrush through my hair, then ran upstairs to look for Tracie. She didn't seem to be in the house, so I started walking next door while calling her name. Tracie emerged from the field behind our house and ran toward me. As she did, I had the odd feeling that someone was watching me. I stopped in the middle of the driveway, slowly turned to look behind me, and saw Dad. He had a longing expression on his face and seemed anxious for me to leave.

"Dad, what are you going to be working on this morning?" I asked, feeling suspicious for reasons I could not even pinpoint.

"I just have some things I need to get done around the house. Now you go on," he said. "And don't forget to take your sister."

I called after Tracie to hurry and come to me.

"What?" she asked in an irritated, six-year-old tone.

"Dad said I have to take you babysitting with me," I groaned.

"Yea!" she happily replied. Tracie always enjoyed playing with the girls next door and "helping" me look after them.

The girls' Mom met me at the door before I could knock. She herded us through the house, giving instructions for the day: a list of phone numbers, snack options, and the lunch menu.

"I'll be home after lunch," she said as she headed out the door.

I watched from Natalie's bedroom window as Mrs. Joy drove away. Then I immediately went to the guest bathroom to look out the window that framed my house. There was no activity at my house. The garage door was shut, the front door was shut, and Dad was nowhere in sight. This seemed odd since he'd told me he had a lot of work to do around the house. That usually meant he would be working in the yard or on the car. If that was the case, the garage door should be open. It was also odd that our front door was shut on a Saturday. On such a beautiful autumn day, the inner door would normally be open to let the fresh air flow through the screen door.

I sat in the kitchen, looking at the newspaper funnies as the kids played house in the basement. Every few minutes I went to the bathroom and looked out the window to see if there was any activity at my house. I called for Tracie to come upstairs and she quickly came running up.

"We don't have anything to eat over here," I lied. "Go home and get some snacks for us."

"Okay," she innocently replied.

Tracie was gone for almost fifteen minutes, as I paced back and forth in the small guest bathroom, peering out the window. Then she came running out the front door, loaded with oranges and apples. I ran to the kitchen and sat back down at the table so I would not look anxious. When she came in, she proudly displayed the fruit. I smiled and thanked her.

As she started to leave the kitchen, to head back downstairs to play with Natalie and Kayla, I casually asked, "What was Daddy doing?"

"He's in the garage getting ready to drive his car to work," she said.

Pure panic now consumed me and I tried not to look nervous or alarm my sister.

"You saw him?" I asked.

"Yes," she said.

"What did he say to you?"

"I asked him for gum and why he had pictures of us in the car. He told me he was taking them to work and to come back over here," she said, now looking at me with curiosity.

I didn't want her to become suspicious and I didn't have the courage to tell her what I was thinking, so I sent her downstairs with a smile and a pat of congratulations for the fruit.

I immediately went to the bathroom window, hoping to find my father in the front yard, but he was not there. The house was shut up tight, as if there was no one home. I managed the courage to call home. As the phone rang, I searched for some excuse for my call, but my father didn't answer. I immediately called Mom at work.

"Hair Design, how can I help you?" a receptionist answered.

"Is Adele in?" I asked.

"Please hold."

I waited.

"This is Adele."

I was very relieved to hear my mother's voice, but I didn't know what to say to her. I didn't know how to tell an adult that I thought another adult might be doing something bad. If I was right about my father sitting in his running car with the garage door shut, I might get Dad in trouble. If I were wrong, Dad would be very angry and disappointed in me for thinking such a horrible thing about him.

"Hello, this is Adele," Mom said again.

"Mom . . ." I said slowly.

"What is it?" she replied, frustrated. "I'm busy."

"Mom . . ." I started again. "Dad is next door, sitting in his car in the garage," I managed to say.

"I'll be right there," Mom said to someone at the salon. "What are you trying to say little girl?" Mom asked, curtly.

My heart was now pounding and I didn't know what else to say. I wanted Mom to read my mind and not make me say it. I wanted her to tell me not to worry and that she would be home right away. I wanted her to reassure me that Dad would never do what I was thinking and it was okay for me to have these thoughts because he had been acting strangely the past few months.

"Carrie Jo, what are you trying to say?" Mom repeated impatiently.

"Just what I said before Mom," I replied sheepishly. "Dad is sitting in the car in our garage." I couldn't manage to say the rest.

"Are you next door babysitting?" she asked.

"Yes." I replied.

"Call your Father," she suggested.

"I did and no one is answering," I said.

"Is Tracie with you?" she asked.

"Yes."

"Go next door and find your Father and have him call me," she ordered.

"Okay," I replied, and I hung up the phone.

I went downstairs to check on the kids. They were happily watching cartoons. I told them I had to run next door for a minute and I would be right back.

My heart still pounding, I forced myself to run to my house and stopped at the front of the driveway. I was breathing hard and overtaken by fear. I slowly walked toward the garage and listened outside the door. My heart sank and I felt queasy as I heard the humming of our car through the garage door. I stood there, trying to muster up the courage to go into the house or look through the windows that lined the top of the garage door. But I couldn't do it. I was afraid I would find my father and he would yell at me to leave him alone.

I ran as fast as I could back to our neighbor's house and back to the kitchen. I riffled through the kitchen desk and found a book and looked up the phone number of the neighbors on the other side of us. Dad and Mr. King were friends. I quickly called him.

"Hello," Mr. King answered.

"Mr. King, this is Carrie and I was wondering if you could do me a favor. I'm babysitting and I need to reach my father. He's not answering the phone. He told me he was working in the garage this morning, so he probably can't hear the phone, so can you go over to our house and tell him I'm trying to call him?" I blurted, without taking a breath.

"Sure," he replied, sounding as if he suspected something. "What's your phone number?"

I hadn't explained that I was right next door to my own house and I didn't want to explain further.

"Oh, uh, I don't know. Tell him I will call him in five minutes while I look for my number," I said, off the cuff.

"Okay," he replied. "I'll let him know."

I felt relief as I hung up the phone. I knew Mr. King would talk some sense into my father and save us both from embarrassment. I ran to the bathroom window and watched Mr. King as he emerged from his house and walked over to our house. He passed the garage, walked up to the front door, and rang the bell. He stood on the front stoop for what seemed an eternity and then slowly walked away. My heart sunk as he started to leave. Then he stopped in front of the garage and stood for a minute. Oh please, oh please, oh please, I thought to myself. Please hear the car. But he didn't, and walked back to his house.

Pure terror consumed me. Mr. King was my last hope. I realized it was now up to me. I stared at our house through the bathroom window and tried to find the courage to open the garage door and confront my father.

Finding Him

Suicide Survivors are the family or friends of a person who dies by suicide. It has been estimated that for every suicide there are at least six related survivors.

October 13, 1979: Mid-morning

Suddenly I felt as if I had become a character in a slow motion movie and was watching myself. I could feel my heart pounding against my chest and hear myself breathing heavily as I walked out of the neighbor's bathroom, down the hall, and right out the front door.

As I approached my own house, my awareness of the world around me heightened. The sky was brighter, the dirt road darker, and my house began to take on a life of its own. At the end of the driveway I could hear the echoing of our car's engine, idling inside the garage. I walked up the concrete drive, past the garage door, and around the pathway to our front door.

I continued to watch myself from a safe distance as I reached out to open the front door and entered the house. I could smell exhaust fumes in the entryway as they pushed their way in from the door connecting the garage to the house.

I watched myself as I stood outside the door to the garage, listening to the purring of the car engine and trying to muster up the courage to open the door and look in. Go on, I coaxed myself. I slowly turned the doorknob.

As I pushed the door open, a thick cloud of smoke, which stung my eyes and pierced my nose, consumed me. I began to choke from the toxic fumes as I stood in the doorway, trying to see through the fog. I hit the garage door opener and as the smoke escaped into the crisp mid-morning fall air, I began to see the car . . . and then my father's head, lying back against the front seat. Life suddenly sped up.

I ran to the car and stopped at the driver's side door, looking at my father as he rested peacefully in the car. I was relieved to find him sleeping instead of the alert person, angry at being disturbed, I pictured in my mind.

I opened the car door and called "Daddy?" in a shaking voice. He did not answer me.

"Daddy, wake up," I said, but he did not move.

The noise of the car began to pound in my head, so I looked for a way to turn off the engine. As I struggled to turn off the engine, I remembered getting into trouble once for messing with the car.

While playing with the car's steering wheel and stick shift as my parents shopped, the car had begun to move through the parking lot. I was scared to death because I didn't know how to stop it. My father had come out in time to run along the side of the car, jump in, and stop it before any damage was done, but he was furious. I had never touched a car since.

I was afraid of making the same mistake this time and feared I would start the car rolling down our driveway instead of turning it off. I decided not to touch the key and turned back to my father.

I grabbed him by his shoulders and shook.

"Daddy," I said, my voice and body trembling. "Wake up, please wake up," I demanded.

I wrapped my arms around my father's chest and slowly dragged him out of the car. When his top half was out of the car, he became too heavy for me and I dropped him on the garage floor. His head hit the ground with a loud thump that echoed in the garage and made my stomach leap.

I felt helpless because I was too weak to finish pulling my father out of the car and too stupid to figure out how to turn the car off.

"Hold on Daddy," I said to my unconscious father, "I'll be right back."

I felt I was moving in slow motion as I ran down our driveway and over to Mr. King's house. I rang the doorbell and tried to find the words to explain what was going on. When Mr. King's wife opened the door, she immediately turned white and asked what was wrong.

"It's Dad," I said fretfully.

Mr. King appeared at the door, towering over Mrs. King. Somehow Mrs. King knew that whatever had happened was serious.

Without asking any more questions she said, "I'll call 911."

Mr. King leapt past me and ran down the road, up our drive, and into our garage. I stood on Mr. King's front stoop and watched as he dragged my father's limp body out of the garage and onto the grass. I could see him yelling at my father, but I couldn't make out what he was saying. Mrs. King startled me when she returned to the door and asked me to come inside. As I stood in her living room, she continued to make calls, including one to my mother at work.

Suddenly I felt as if a jolt of lightning had hit me and awakened me from the dreamlike state I had been in. The children, I thought to myself.

"Mrs. King, I'm babysitting Natalie and Kayla. I better go check in on them," I said, concerned.

"Well, okay," Mrs. King hesitantly replied.

I dashed out the door and ran past my house and on to Natalie's and Kayla's house. As I ran by, I caught a quick glance of Mr. King hovering over my father.

When I got to the house, I went downstairs to check on the kids. They were still playing in the basement. Tracie asked if she could have a snack. I told her she could and that I would get it for her.

I ran back upstairs and into the now familiar guest bathroom, to peer out the window and see what was happening at my house. I saw the bright, flashing lights of emergency vehicles, parked in front of the house. I saw people in white shirts and dark pants crowded around the lawn.

The neighbors began to gather on the road in front of my house and I was horrified to think that this event might be on the news. I wondered what people would think. I wondered what I would say if a reporter asked me questions. I wondered what would happen to our family if my father became a vegetable or had brain damage for the rest of his life.

I heard the door to the house open and I ran to the entryway to see my mother standing there, stiff and pale. I sat down on the couch and she positioned herself beside me, placing her hand gently on my knee. A man in uniform followed behind her and sat down on the coffee table directly in front of us. He began to ask us questions.

"What is your husband's name?" the man asked my mom.

Mom just sat, staring blankly ahead.

"Cameron John Stark," I quietly replied.

He nodded and wrote down my response.

"How old is he?" he asked, looking at my mother.

"Thirty-eight," I answered with my mom nodding in agreement.

"Mom, I'll be right back, I have to go to the bathroom," I lied.

"Okay," Mom said with a gentle pat on my leg.

I ran down the hall and into the bathroom to look out the window just in time to see a group of people elevate a table with a large white cloth draped over it. I saw that it was covering my father's dead body as they began to roll him into the ambulance.

The reality behind the image of my father covered up on the stretcher began to sink in. I couldn't quite sort out all my feelings because they were hitting me both quickly and simultaneously. I recognized a feeling of relief that my father was not a vegetable and did not have brain damage. Then I felt fear as I thought about my sister and me being alone. I felt embarrassment that the neighbors were hovering outside my house, whispering and gossiping about my family and me. Guilt and shame were added to the melting pot as

I thought of what could have happened if I had only had the courage to go to my father sooner. At the same time, I was confused about why my father had done this to himself and why I wasn't crying about it. My stomach trembled and my head pounded as I tried to sort through what was happening.

I went back to the living room and sat on the couch with my mother, observing the commotion around me. I became so weigh down by my thoughts and feelings, as well as all the activity; I finally asked my mother if I could go downstairs. She agreed, nodding as if in a trance.

I slowly walked away from the commotion, escaped to the basement, turned on the television, and tried to lose myself in the familiarity of James T. Kirk getting frustrated by Tribbles. I had watched this *Star Trek* episode with my father a dozen times. I stretched out on the neighbor's couch and tucked a pillow under my head, pretending it was my father's comforting lap—a lap I knew I would never again rest on.

The Aftermath

The stigma that surrounds a suicide or suicide attempt often causes survivors to avoid talking about their experience, which can result in profound isolation, as well as a unique grief that can include guilt, anger, shame or embarrassment.

—Suicide Prevention Action Network, USA

October 13, 1979: Afternoon

Tracie and the kids were still playing in the basement and had no idea what was going on upstairs. After I watched James T. Kirk save the galaxy, I decided to go back upstairs and check in on my own reality.

Tammy and her boyfriend Jim were sitting next to Mom on the couch. Just then, Mrs. Joy entered the commotion of police officers and paramedics coming in and out of the house. She seemed worried, concerned, and upset. I couldn't tell if these emotions were for her children or me.

The ambulance, helicopter, and fire trucks had already left, and since there was nothing more to watch, the neighbors had gone back to their homes. Tracie came upstairs and asked Mom and Tammy what they were doing there. Mom grabbed Tracie's hand and we all walked back to the house in silence.

I sat in the dining room while Mom led Tracie back to her bedroom and shut the door. Several minutes later I heard Tracie begin to sob and I knew Mom had broken the news. I knew it would be difficult for Mom to explain all of this to a six-year-old little kid. Tracie kept asking Mom over and over, "Why, didn't Daddy stay for my birthday?"

I went to my room to cocoon myself against the events of the day. Instead, pure panic enveloped me when I started to think of my friends at school and what they would say and think of me. Seventh grade was already tough enough.

I had been with the same group of kids throughout primary school. Making friends had always been easy. But the classes in middle school were bigger. There were more faces and people to get to know. I had only been in my new school for six weeks and was still trying to work my way into the cool crowd. I groaned inwardly, realizing that this would make fitting in even more difficult. I felt heat rise up into my face and was consumed with embarrassment. I couldn't imagine how I was going to face the kids at school.

"Dad how could you do this to me?" I moaned out loud in frustration.

Then my inner thoughts took over. "Shame on you!" a voice said inside. "Your father is dead and all you can think about is your popularity!"

I sat on my bed, wrestling with my ego and conscience, until I heard footsteps above me. I went to the bottom of the steps and heard the voices of my aunt, uncle, and grandmothers.

We called my mother's mom Maga because Tammy couldn't quite pronounce the word "grandma" when she was little and the name stuck. Maga was a very practical woman who didn't much care for kids. She was hard and a little crude. Her favorite shirt was black, with images of fried eggs on the front covering each breast. She enjoyed drinking, smoking, and the horse track. I'd never had a conversation with her because she told me to go outside and play and not to come home until dinner every time she visited.

Once, while working on a school project, I made the mistake of asking her about my heritage.

I asked, "What am I?"

Maga turned sharply and replied, "What the hell do you think you are? You are a goddamn American."

I wasn't quiet sure how to report this to my teacher.

I knew that my grandmother was not a warm or comforting person and I wanted to hear what she and others had to say as they questioned my mother. I sat on the bottom step, eavesdropping.

"So Carrie found him in the car!" exclaimed my aunt Gail.

"Yes she did," snapped my mother, "and I don't want any of you talking to her about it or asking her any questions. I mean it. Don't you dare talk to her about anything," she repeated sternly.

I decided to come upstairs and could feel the tension as I entered the room. Honoring my mother's request, no one spoke to me.

"Mom, can I go play at Cindy's house?" I asked.

"Of course you can," she said, with a reassuring hug.

As I headed out the door, Tammy said, "Wait up. I'll walk you over."

Cindy lived up the hill and across the field. It was a bit of a walk and I nervously wondered what Tammy wanted, knowing she would not have joined me if she hadn't wanted something.

As we walked along the dirt road, my sister disobeyed my mother's order to not talk to me about Dad's death. But disobeying my mother was what Tammy did best.

"Did Dad have something hanging out of his mouth?" asked Tammy.

I wondered where she was going with such a question and replied, "No."

"Did you see a photo album in the car?" she asked.

I was even more confused.

"No," I said again.

"Did you find a note?" she probed.

I shook my head.

"Are you sure you didn't see a tube of some kind or pictures in the car?" she pushed.

Her tone made me panicky.

"No," I said again.

"What did he say to you this morning?"

"Nothing," I replied. "He just told me to take Tracie with me to the neighbors."

I couldn't bring myself to tell her I had suspicions earlier that day. She would never forgive me for failing to stop or rescue him.

"Did you know that Mom and Dad were separated?"

I wondered what she was talking about and shook my head.

"Dad took me apartment shopping a few weeks ago," she reported. "We had one of the best talks we've had in a long time."

I was not prepared to hear this. My mind was spinning and I began to feel light headed.

We reached the top of the dirt road.

"I can manage from here," I yelled as I ran away from her through the field and towards the safety of Cindy's house.

Before I could ring the doorbell Mrs. Rivers opened the door.

"My poor girl!" she exclaimed as she scooped me into her arms, accidentally stepping on my foot in the process.

"Oh, my god!" she exclaimed again. "I can't believe I just stepped on your foot. I'm so sorry. You just lost your Dad, you've been through so much, and I step on your foot. I'm so clumsy! Are you all right? I can't believe I did this."

Cindy finally came down the stairs to rescue me from her mother, who continued to apologize for stepping on my foot, even though I hadn't even felt her do it. It was just nice to have someone's arms around me and I was willing to hear her continue to go on about the foot, just to feel the security of her arms. She released me. Cindy and I went upstairs to her bedroom while Mrs. Rivers recapped the tragedy of my father's death for Mr. Rivers.

I was instantly comforted by the familiar surroundings of Cindy's room. We had spent much time together in this room, listening to records, playing with dolls, and talking all night when I slept over. Cindy had a beautiful lace canopy bed and a bathroom that connected to her bedroom. I so loved and admired her room.

We didn't talk much, which was unusual for us, and I found myself trying to fade away into memories of our friendship.

Cindy's birthday was on New Year's Eve. Each New Year's Eve, for as long as I could remember, several girls had slept over at her house. We stayed up late, watching Dick Clark count down the time to the next year, and after the ball dropped in Time Square, we randomly called people in the phone book and screamed, "Happy New Year!" Then we turned out the lights, lit candles, and played our favorite game, "Light as a feather, stiff as a board."

Those memories sustained me for a time, as Cindy and I just sat together, but I eventually had to return to my own home, my own bed, and a feeling of profound aloneness.

October 14, 1979

I awoke the next morning with an emptiness I had never felt before. I heard the voices of friends and strangers flowing through the house. Our kitchen counters and refrigerator were filled with casseroles, food trays, and cakes, brought by well-meaning friends and neighbors who did not know what else to do. I had never seen so much food in my life, not even at Christmas.

Just as the food had appeared without warning, strange people also began to arrive. My mother had an older brother named Ed, who I had never before met. He stood awkwardly in the living room of our house with his new wife.

"You remember your uncle Ed don't you Carrie?" asked my mother, as I stared at him with a blank expression on my face.

Grandma Stark sat on the couch, looking confused and upset. "Where is Jack?" she kept asking. "I need to talk with Jack."

Jack was the name Grandma had called Dad since he was a child. She was a devout Catholic and although she didn't come right out and say it, I was pretty sure she was worried that her son was in Hell for the act he had committed the previous day. Mom tried, without much success, to comfort and calm Grandma.

I felt as if I were in one of the *Twilight Zone* shows I'd watched with Dad. I wanted to wake up and find that things were exactly as they had been days or weeks ago. Everyone around me was unrecognizable. Their actions and words were unfamiliar to me. I felt suffocated and wanted out. I wanted things to be back to the way they were before; back to being normal.

The Funeral

Children have the same emotional needs after the suicide of a loved one as adults, but often their hurts are not taken seriously. Many times adults have their hands full of grief and do not think to reach out to the children.

—Hope for Bereaved, Inc.

October 17, 1979

I had never been to a funeral before. My grandfather had died three years earlier, but I had not attended his funeral. I had asked and been granted permission to go to school instead. I wasn't sure what to wear to a funeral or how to act. In the movies they wore big black hats with black veils. I didn't have a hat or a veil, so I decided to put on my best dress and hoped it would be all right.

Few words were spoken as we drove to the chapel. When we entered the small white church, I saw that Dad's coffin sat—closed—at the front of the sanctuary. Thank you, God! I thought. I had seen movies of funerals where the casket was open and the dead body was in view for all to see. I did not want to see my father that way.

We walked to the front of the church and sat in the front row. I stared at the gray box, trying to imagine my father lying in there. The pastor said a few words and my mother went to kneel by the coffin. She caressed it with her right hand, then kissed her hand and pressed it against the box.

As I listened to the pastor and watched my mother at the coffin, I thought the tears would finally come, but nothing happened. I didn't feel like crying. I wondered what was wrong with me. Why couldn't I cry? Would people think I didn't love my dad? Would they think something was wrong with me?

When Mom sat back down after saying good-bye to Dad, everyone got up from their seats and came over to us with hugs, kisses, and words of sorrow. This made me very uncomfortable. I didn't know these people, and I disliked their pitying stares.

We rode in a limo to the cemetery. It was the first time I had been in a limo and I was very curious about all of the buttons. One button opened the windows, another turned on the radio, and one made the partition behind the driver go up and down. There was a long line of cars behind us and we were led by a police escort to stop the traffic and let our funeral convoy pass.

Since Dad served in the army, he was buried with full colors. I wasn't sure what that meant. The cemetery was perfectly groomed and all the headstones were consistent in shape, size, and color. At the top of each headstone was a cross, engraved into the white marble.

We sat in chairs surrounding Dad's coffin, which was adorned with the U.S. flag. Several men in uniform were close by, standing perfectly straight and tall. The pastor said some words. The soldiers shot their guns into the sky, then neatly folded up the flag and gave it to my mother. And with that, the funeral was over. We drove away, leaving my father in his shiny gray box to be buried under the ground.

Once again our house was filled with people and food. I hated the way everyone kept looking at me, their faces full of pity, concern, and judgment. There was nowhere to escape and the behavior of several family members and friends was disturbing. Grandma Stark seemed confused, asking where my father was. I walked in on my sister smoking a joint with one of her friends. My uncle Fred was staggering around drunk, spilling beer all over the carpet. It all seemed bizarre and crazy. I wondered when the madness would end.

In Search of Normal

Children may not show grief by crying, being sad or behaving as we might expect. In fact, continuing their routine play or activities may be the best way the child knows to control and reduce confusing and frightening feelings.

—Vickie Sampson, Vice President
Friends for Survival

October 18, 1979

I asked Mom if I could go back to school the next day and she said I could. As I was getting dressed that morning, all I could think about was getting back to a day of being normal. I wanted a normal schedule, around my normal friends, at my normal school. I took one last look in the mirror and decided I looked normal.

I sat with Cindy on our thirty-minute bus ride. The familiarity of just riding the bus to school felt good.

But when I entered school, I could tell things were going to be far from normal. Kids were whispering and pointing at me as I walked by them to my locker. I pretended not to notice. I sat down in my first class of the day, English. Not long after class started my friend Molly entered the classroom and asked my teacher if she could have a word with me. I wondered what Molly was doing, what she wanted, but my teacher did not question the reason for the interruption. With a compassionate tone of voice and warm smile, she agreed to let me leave the room.

Out in the hallway Molly began to drill me with questions about the weekend. I answered her as directly as I could, in short words or sentences. Our conversation was drawing way too much attention to me and was not part of the normal routine I was so desperately seeking.

"So, why didn't he just take a gun and go shoot himself in the field so you wouldn't have to find him?" she asked me.

I could scarcely believe she would ask me such a question. I found myself picturing a horrible image of my father lying in the alfalfa fields behind our house, in his own blood. I shook off the visual.

"Molly, I really need to get back to class," I said, almost begging.

Back at my locker between classes, two boys I didn't know came up to me and started teasing me about my dad. They chanted, saying horrible things like "your dad is crazy" and "only crazy people kill themselves." I was shocked by their statements and wanted them to go away because they were drawing unwanted attention to me.

As I stood there, paralyzed, a small eighth grade girl approached the boys and began telling them off. I was stunned by her beautiful olive complexion, confidence, and accurate use of swear words. Within minutes, she had the boys leaving, holding back tears. I had never seen anything like it in my life. Then she turned her attention toward me. I held my breath as I waited to see what she would say.

"The next time those jerks or anyone else gives you a hard time about your dad," she said, addressing her comments to me and making eye contact with both me and the other kids who had gathered to watch, "you just tell them to fuck off."

She gently patted my arm and walked away. I couldn't believe she used the "F" word. I stood there dumbfounded, then slowly walked to my next class.

That was the beginning of my friendship with Nicole. She became my best friend and my biggest advocate. Being with her gave me power and hanging out with her made me feel very cool. I envied her beauty, feistiness, and directness. I had never met anyone like her before. She knew how to stand up for herself and others.

Nicole's parents had just gotten separated. Her father wasn't around much and her mother was out very late most nights at parties or on dates. Nicole was the youngest child and her older brothers and sister had already moved out of the house. We spent most of our time at her house, so we could be alone. We stayed up most of the night calling boys, listening to Billy Joel albums, and reenacting *Grease*.

At school, things continued to be difficult for me. The school counselor asked me to join a grief group with other seventh and eighth grade students who had lost a parent. It was presented to me as if I didn't have a choice. I was nervous about the first meeting. There were about six of us and I was relieved to see that one of the popular boys in the eighth grade, a friend of Nicole, was also in the group.

Everyone in the group shared how their parent had died.

Each talked of feelings of sadness, anger, and loss. It seemed to me that all the other parents had died normally, from things like cancer and car accidents.

When it was my turn, I didn't know what to say. I was not like these people. My dad did not die normally. Suicide was not natural. I wasn't sure how I felt, but knew I had feelings I wanted to run away from, feelings that frightened me. They didn't feel like sadness, anger, or loss. I didn't know exactly what they were. All I knew was that I was going to out run them and not let them swallow me up. No one knew what this was like. How could anyone understand what I was going through? I sat quietly through every session saying as little as possible and trying to be invisible.

Coping

Suicide is different. On top of all the grief that people experi-ence after a "conventional" death, you must walk a gauntlet of guilt, confusion and emotional turmoil that is in many ways unique to survivors of suicide.

—Jeffrey Jackson, American Association of Suicidology,
Handbook for Suicide Survivors

Winter 1980

Each night Tracie asked the same three questions about Dad when Mom tucked her into bed.

"Where did Daddy go? When will he come back? Why didn't he stay for my birthday?"

My mom always looked drained after completing this nightly routine. Then she shut herself away in her room. Sometimes I peeked through the keyhole and found her sitting on the floor, sitting upright but with her legs pulled up and her arms tucked around them, as if in an upright fetal position. Looking like a frightened child, she stared at the wall. My mother had always behaved confidently and had managed the household with skill and precision. Seeing my mother afraid made me afraid that she might decide to leave like Dad. I began a suicide watch, stalking her night and day to make sure she was all right.

"Are you okay?" I often asked her.

"Yes, honey," she always replied.

One night I found Mom slumped over in her green chair. Sitting beside her was a glass and a bottle of wine.

"Are you okay?" I asked.

"Yes, honey," she replied, looking at me with half-moon-shaped eyes.

I had never seen my mother drink before. Dad had often had a beer or two while working in the yard, but I had never seen either of my parents drunk.

Late afternoon each day I developed a dull pain in my head that would last until bedtime. No amount of aspirin, food, or rest would make it go away. Headaches became part of my daily routine.

I was also constantly tired. I could fall asleep at any time and in any place. Sleep was my escape from my new reality. At first I was afraid to sleep, afraid that the events of the day Dad died would haunt me in my dreams. I was pleasantly surprised to find my dreams peaceful and comforting. Many times I found myself back in my father's arms in my dreams, with everyone around me acting as they had before his suicide.

Mom had arranged for the entire family to see a counselor. Mom always went in first and when she was done it was my turn. I often fell asleep in the waiting room before I had to face the counselor, which felt like facing a firing squad. I wasn't sure what to say to this person. During my first encounter with her she asked if I was angry at Dad. I thought this was an odd question because it had never crossed my mind.

"No," I replied.

"Yes you are," she replied, "you just don't know it yet."

I was taken aback by her response. It seemed that all my responses to Dad's death were considered wrong. I hadn't yet cried and was not mad at him. From that point forward I thought it best to say as little as possible to the counselor.

There was a constant feeling of anger floating throughout the house. The feeling was strongest around my dad's bar, which unfortunately was located in the game room next to my bedroom. This was one of my father's most cherished possessions. Grandpa had crafted the bar out of beautiful wood and it looked like something from the old west. There were four high stools in front. Mirrors with glass shelves lined the walls behind the bar. On the shelves were steins and miniature glass animals filled with colored liqueurs that my father had collected when he was stationed in Germany. There were illuminated Budweiser signs and a real cash register. The bar was once a place filled with pride and joy . . . but it felt cold and angry now that Dad was gone.

I had to walk past the bar to reach my bedroom. Each night I took a deep breath as I started through the game room. I always began walking at a fast pace, but sprinted as I passed the bar. Then I would dive into my bedroom, lock my door, jump into bed, and pull the covers over my head.

The bathroom adjacent to my room had a connecting door to the bar area. Every morning, while I showered, I stared at the door because it always felt as if someone was lurking on the other side.

One night I got the courage to stop in front of the bar and stand for a minute to confirm the feelings I was having. I then walked around the bar and made myself stand in the center, surrounded by the glass animal figures and steins. I stood there shaking, a feeling of fear and anger penetrating me. For a moment I could not move, talk, or scream.

Then I heard myself say, "Dad, it's me. Are you angry at me?"

There was no response and my fear grew stronger. I bolted out of the bar, into my bedroom, and under the covers of my bed. I felt my heart pounding as I lay in bed wondering if Dad was okay.

I had always believed in Heaven. I pictured myself one day floating with the angels in the clouds, eating as much ice cream as I wanted, and laughing nonstop. If Dad was so angry, then it seemed to me he couldn't be in heaven. I had been baptized Catholic and knew all about the teachings of God and the Devil, from the Catholic perspective. I often worried that my thoughts and actions would put me in the fiery depths at the core of the earth, hammering away at black rocks on a chain gang, feeling sad and scared.

The feelings I experienced in Dad's special bar area were those of anger, not sadness or fear. I wondered if he was in Purgatory, that space Catholics believe is between Heaven and Hell. I pictured Dad on a small deserted island with one palm tree for shade, surrounded by miles and miles of water. I thought that God might not yet have decided what to do with him or that he might be in a special place where people go when they kill themselves. I had been taught that killing yourself was a sin. I couldn't bear the thought of Dad on a chain gang with the Devil.

"Please forgive my dad," I pleaded with God.

I tried to remind God of all the wonderful things my father had done while he was alive.

"He used to give us rides on his back; he let me lie on his lap while watching television; he was very funny and told great jokes; he gave great hugs and he loved me, Lord, I know he did. Please, please, please don't send him to Hell. I will do anything you want," I prayed as I escaped to my peaceful place of slumber.

In Debt

Someone you love has ended their own life—and yours is forever changed.

—Jeffrey Jackson, American Association of Suicidology,
Handbook for Suicide Survivors

Spring 1980

During my daily suicide watch over Mom, I often listened in on her telephone conversations. It was in this way that I discovered we were in serious financial trouble. One day I overheard her crying on the phone, as she talked with Maga. She said that we had so many unpaid bills that collectors were beginning to call. She wanted to put the house up for sale but she had discovered that Aunt Joan had placed a lien on it, which meant it could not be sold. She told Maga that Aunt Joan, my father's only sister, was suing us on behalf of Grandma Stark because Aunt Joan believed her mother had a financial interest in our house.

Aunt Joan also wanted full custody of Grandma Stark, all her belongings, and money from my father's estate.

"Why was she doing this to us?" my mother asked Maga.

I had always been a little fearful of Aunt Joan. She and Mom had never gotten along and I thought that Aunt Joan was jealous of my father in some way. We lived in a nicer house than she did and Grandma Stark treated Dad nicer than her. Aunt Joan always appeared unhappy and always seemed to think that someone was out to get her. My parents had often had conversations about Aunt Joan threatening, or in the process of suing, someone over something.

Over the months that followed the phone conversation about money, Mom cried more at nights and seemed more stressed than ever. There was a "for sale" sign on our house and people kept coming to see it. Mom had offered Aunt Joan a deal that would surrender any rights to Grandma Stark and her belongings if she would remove the lien from the house. When the bank was about to foreclose on the house, Aunt Joan accepted the offer, fearing that she would lose everything otherwise.

My mother packed and loaded up all of Grandma's things in the back of a moving truck. Uncle Fred, and the new cousin I met after Dad died, drove the truck with me to a meeting place. Aunt Joan had a detailed list and checked off each item as it was removed from the truck and placed on the lawn.

"Carrie Jo!" she screamed. I jumped. "Where are Grandma's ruby earrings?"

I had no idea what she was talking about. I shrugged my shoulders. I was sitting on the ground far from her reach and stayed put.

"You tell your mother I expect to get those earrings, you hear!"

Uncle Fred's chest ballooned up. "You have everything that was in the apartment. Now let us be!" he exclaimed as he came over to me, grabbed my hand, and led me to the truck. We drove away without another word.

I had hoped that Grandma Stark would be at the meeting place because I hadn't seen her since the funeral. Mom had told me that Aunt Joan had put Grandma in a nursing home for old people so she could be cared for properly. Aunt Joan had put her in a state hospital and Mom was not happy about this. Mom wanted Grandma to be in a private hospital because she thought she would receive better care there.

I worried about Grandma. She was still physically present, but when you looked into her eyes, she was gone. I wondered where she had gone and if she would ever come back to us because I missed playing cards with her.

Our house sold and this was a huge relief to me. The constancy of our family problems had left me with a perpetual headache. I awoke with a dull ache and the only time I had relief was when I slept.

We had only a few weeks to find a new home and move our things. Over the past several months, Mom had found homes for all our pets. Our horses went to another ranch and the dogs found homes with neighbors. With all the changes in our lives, Mom wanted at least one thing to remain constant for us, so she promised to find a house in the same school district. That way, we wouldn't have to change schools. This was a big relief for me because the kids were finally forgetting about what had happened to my dad and I was just starting to feel like I fit in.

It wasn't long before we found the perfect house. It was within walking distance of our schools and had three bedrooms. Even though it was much smaller than the house we'd been living in, I thought it was much prettier.

Although I was sad to move, I looked forward to leaving the angry vibes of our current house. I wondered if Dad and his anger would follow us to the new house or if he would stay and haunt the new people moving in.

I began to plan how I would decorate my bedroom and I looked forward to walking to school instead of taking the long bus ride over the dirt road. It felt as if there was a little bit of light finally shining on us after a long period of darkness.

A New Normal

And my heart goes out to those who are left behind, because I know that they suffer terribly. Children in particular are left under a cloud of "differentness" all the more terrifying because it can never be fully explained or lifted. The immediate family of the victim is left wide open to tidal waves of guilt "What did I fail to do that I should have done? What did I do that was wrong?"

—Norman Vincent Peale, *The Healing of Sorrow: Understanding and Help for the Bereaved*

October 13, 1980

It is amazing how time stops when a loved one dies. I feel that a part of me will forever be that scared little girl who found him: embarrassed by her father's death, ashamed that she didn't have the courage to stop him, and constantly in search of a normal life.

There may always be a part of me that is afraid to feel or show sadness, for I fear it might overwhelm and swallow me whole as it did my father. I hope not. I will perpetually regret that I could not give

Dad the tears he deserved in death and continue to resent those judging eyes at his funeral that couldn't understand.

My father may continue to be a mystery to me, one I protect, hide, and defend. I may forever see him through confused girl's eyes and cling to memories and images of him. My father's attributes continue to fade in my mind with each passing day. I can hardly remember how he smells or what he feels like. There are times when the details of his face begin to fade and I hold his picture, desperately tracing ever crack and detail so I will not forget him.

Dad will forever be thirty-eight years old to me. I will never see him gray and wrinkled, which makes me feel as if my universe will always be misplaced and somehow out of order. When I grow up, I will never be able to see him through a woman's eyes. He will miss my graduations from high school and college and will never be there to walk me down the isle on my wedding day. I dread the day I must tell my future husband about my father, and I dread even more that I will one day have to tell my children about their grandfather's suicide.

The craziest and scariest thing of all is that I have now learned there is a way to break the laws of nature. I never before realized that to live was a choice and not an absolute. Suicide has now become one of the options for me to choose from when I feel dragged down by life's challenges—a lesson well taught to me by my father. And death is now something that is unnatural, fearful, and my enemy.

It has been a year now since that day we were abandoned by my father. Although the wound my father inflicted on me has stopped bleeding, I now know the scab will leave a massively deep scar that will mark me for the rest of my life. Pain still consumes my head daily and I desperately wish I had the courage and strength to uncork my tears, for I know this would bring me great relief.

My suicide counselor told me that the body and mind has powerful survival instincts. She said that because I was so emotionally injured by my father's death, the only way I could comprehend it was for my mind to write down all my thoughts and feelings, as if on a piece of paper I store in my back pocket for safe keeping. She told me that when I am ready, my mind would take out this piece of paper so I can resolve each item on the list, one at a time.

Tracie's mind and body has reacted in a different way to Dad's death. She hasn't physically grown since the day Dad died. Mom took her to the doctor to make sure she was okay. The doctor told Mom that this was common for children who endure the stress of losing a parent. The impact of Dad's death stopped Tracie's mind and body from producing her growth hormone. I guess a part of her will always be that little girl searching for the answer to her question, "Why didn't Daddy stay for my birthday?"

As I lie in bed in my new bedroom, I realize that for the first time in a long time I feel safe. My father's ghost didn't follow us to the new house and no longer haunts me. I think he is stuck at the old house. Mom went to see a psychic and she said that when someone kills himself, he is stuck in a cold, dark, and confused place. She told Mom that Dad's unsettled spirit was roaming through our old home in pain, impacted by the reality of what he did. She said that Dad was very angry.

I wonder how long he will be stuck there before he can move on to the next passage of his existence . . . and I hope it will be Heaven.

That old saying, "You can't see the forest for the trees," is so true. Looking back, I didn't see the signs Dad and my gut were sending in any collective way that rose to the level of consciousness. I can remember each sign so clearly now, but they never added up to anything until it was too late. And even then, I kept thinking I was wrong.

We continue to try to pick up the pieces of our lives day by day. Mom brought home two cats for Tracie and me last week. Tracie named her black tabby cat Cuddles, which I think is a pretty dumb name, and I named my orange and white calico Tiggers. It's nice to have animals around the house again, although I miss the horses and dogs. I wonder if they are happy in their new homes and if they think of me on occasion.

I am now in eighth grade. The boys grew bigger over the summer. So did some of the girls. I'm no longer the tallest girl in my grade. I tried out for track this year and have volunteered as a trainer for the wrestling team.

I live closer to my school friends now, although I don't see them much. Mom work's full time in the hair salon and I spend my time after school and on weekends taking care of Tracie. But Nicole sometimes came over this summer. We sun bathed, laying on top of our trampoline to catch some rays, and then walked down to the Seven Eleven for a Big Gulp. Often we watched *Days of Our Lives* on television, and then mustered up the courage to call the boys we liked. It was fun.

Mom doesn't usually get home until after dinner. Sometimes her feet and ankles are so swollen from standing all day, that I spend the evening rubbing them for her. Mom is up early each morning, before Tracie and I are awake, to get ready and head off to work again. She usually leaves us a list of chores to do around the house and yard, along with one of the casseroles from the freezer, which she makes on Sundays. Tracie and I are expected to call her every day when we get home from school, to check in.

Tracie has become a magnet for all the little kids in our new neighborhood. It doesn't matter if the kid is two or ten; she gets everyone to participate and leads the pack in various games all day. New kids are always dropping by and asking if Tracie can play. Mom says Tracie will grow up to be a teacher or have some kind of career working with children.

Tammy and Mom still don't get along and now communicate through me. Mom tells me to call my sister and ask her to come over for dinner, and then Tammy calls and asks me to tell Mom she is going to Europe with her new boyfriend, Ted . . . and on it goes.

This odd form of conversation has actually made my sister and me closer this past year. We don't fight anymore and I have started to confide in Tammy and ask for advice. The nice thing about having a wild sister is that you can tell her anything because she has either done it or knows of someone who has.

All in all, Mom, my sisters, and I are surviving. In a strange way, Dad's death has made us all closer to each other and created a bond that no one will ever be able to break or understand. We don't speak to outsiders about Dad or share our feelings. He has become the family secret that is kept tightly locked within our foursome.

People sometimes ask where my father is or if my parents are divorced. When I tell them my father is dead, the response is always the same: a dreaded pause and then the inevitable question, "How did he die?" I tried honesty a few times, but the reaction I saw on the faces of the people I told made me abandon the honest approach. It is hard enough for people to understand that you are a girl with no father, but a father who committed suicide is unbelievable. I don't doubt that they have trouble understanding it when I'm still struggling to understand it myself. These days I lie when people ask me how my father died. I tell them he had cancer or something else considered respectable as a cause of death. Sometimes if they catch me in a bad mood, I tell them it is none of their damn business. Or to invoke sympathy, I will say I don't really want to talk about it.

It's amazing to think back to the person I was a year ago and then see the new person I am today. It's as if I was forced out of the warm, safe womb of innocence and pushed into a harsh reality. That harsh reality is the undependable world I live in today. The impact of my father's suicide has transformed me. I will always miss and long for the girl who played in the alfalfa fields and laid her head on her father's lap while watching TV. I can honestly say that I have experienced two births in my life: the first on October 8, 1966, and another, thirteen years later, on October 13, 1979.

Epilogue

As of the completion of this book it's been twenty-nine years since the suicide death of my father. I went on to graduate from high school, earned a Bachelor of Arts degree in public relations, married a wonderful man, and birthed two beautiful children.

Through my walk of pain I didn't always make the healthiest choices. During my teen years I coped by drinking excessively and experimenting with drugs. When these approaches did not alleviate the pain, I turned to teachers and counselors in college for help. During the past two decades, therapists helped me sort through new and unexpected feelings about my father's suicide (my subconscious did keep that list of complicated feelings in my back pocket after all).

Even now, the longing for my father is still with me and I think of him every day. I miss his smile, laughing eyes, sense of humor, and playful spirit. The pain of his death slowly subsided and was replaced with more and more memories of his life.

Dad's suicide, although a large piece of me, has not been the main focus of my life. Since his death I have laughed much, enjoyed both personal and professional successes, and taken pleasure in my favorite activities.

I've survived the suicide death of my father and come out the other side living a new normal—a life filled with joy, love, beautiful children, a supporting family, and wonderful friends.

Grief Support Tips

Helping Adolescents through Grief

Children experience many of the feelings of adult grief, and are particularly vulnerable to feeling abandoned and guilty. Reassure them that the death was not their fault. Listen to their questions, and try to offer honest, straightforward, age-appropriate answers.

—American Foundation for Suicide Prevention

A young person who has experienced the loss of a loved one to suicide often experiences complicated grieving. They feel as if time has stopped and life stands still because they are unable to express what happened. To cope, the normal grief responses (such as shock, denial, sadness, anger, guilt, etc.) can be put on hold by the child and they become disconnected from their feelings. Unexpressed grief can contribute to behaviors of bullying, violence, abuse, and homicide or feelings of self-hatred, victimization, low self-esteem, depression, and thoughts of suicide. To help a child unlock and connect to their emotions, encourage them to talk openly about their loved one and the suicide death.

Several years after the suicide death of my father, I started to trust more people with my feelings. I began to learn that asking for help was not a sign of weakness or that I was going to suffer the fate of my father. Once I realized this and began stating my needs, I entered my process of healing. I saw counselors, attended a survivors' support group through HEARTBEAT and I began journaling. Writing this book was also another step in expressing my feelings and helping me heal.

Remind adolescents that there are not good or bad feelings and that there is not a right or wrong way to grieve. Explain that grief is unique to each individual. I often felt like something was wrong with me after my dad died because I was not mourning the way they did in the movies. I did not cry or have an emotional breakdown. This concerned me greatly, and I often felt guilty and cruel for not giving my father the tears he deserved. I've learned that circumstances impact how we grieve and everyone grieves differently. It may also take time for a child to sort through and understand the feelings of grief. In my personal experience this process went well into my adult years as my emotional maturity grew.

Give teenagers room to grieve, but not so much room that they feel abandoned. Your absence will be noticed and your presence will provide security. My biggest fear was that I was going to suddenly become crazy like my father and kill myself. I was scared to face his death and grieve for him because I thought the sorrow would swallow me up. Once I got the courage to sort through my painful feelings I realized I would not go crazy and I began to heal.

Convey that you care and that it's all right to talk about the suicide by using phrases such as, "I'm sorry to hear about your loss," "How are you doing?" or "I'm here when you need me." I wanted to talk openly about my father's death, but there weren't many people who wanted to listen. I often felt that the topic of suicide was too uncomfortable for people so I was left feeling as if they didn't want to know about this side of me. It was as if I was split into two people, the public persona who was "normal" and didn't discuss my father's death and the secret side who was the "un-normal" suicide survivor.

Be sure to help adolescents to not feel guilty for taking care of themselves with rest, eating regularly, drinking water, and getting exercise. It took me many years to master this concept. I would always take care of others before myself because I thought if I took better care of my father he would have stayed. Now I spend time each day being kind to myself. This means moving my body, fueling it with the right foods, and spending time doing my favorite activities (reading, watching movies, being with friends and family). In my opinion, self-kindness is one of the quickest ways to help anyone heal.

Remember that a child who has lost a loved one to suicide may need support over a period of time (even years). Phases in life, including accomplishments, holidays, birthdays, and the anniversary death of the loved one may trigger unexpected feelings. I still think of my father on the day of the anniversary of his death. It was an Indian Summer when my father died and if the weather mirrors that on his anniversary it has a bigger impact on me—the smells and sounds of the magpie's song can bring on sudden and powerful memories. The pain never completely goes away, but it's not as penetrating as it was in the early years. Christmas in general can bring emotions of stress and heartache for many and I'm no exception. These feelings are intensified because my father was born on Christmas day. I still think of him every afternoon when we used to celebrate his birthday. I'm extra kind to myself during this time of the year. I say no to the hustle and bustle of life and slow down to help lessen the emotional impact. I only read and watch uplifting stories. Movies are a great escape for me this time of the year.

Never say to a suicide survivor, "Did you see it coming?" "Why?" "It was God's will," "Suicide is a sin," "I know how you feel," or "Aren't you over this by now?" Guilt can be one of the biggest issues a survivor has to overcome and these types of phrases can add fuel to the fire. Self-forgiveness is easier said than done and I developed a habit of unhealthy self-talk. I would call myself horrible names and criticize most of my actions. It took me several years as an adult to reprogram my self-hatred talk. I began each day looking in the mirror and saying to myself "Carrie, I love you." This was awkward at first, but got easier with time. Once the self-love was established the self-forgiveness came easier.

By no means assume that you know best or how a survivor is feeling by making caparisons to your own losses, and don't tell them how they should feel or try and change their feelings. After my father passed, family, counselors, teachers, and friends would tell me what or how I should feel. Most of the time they were wrong, which added to my confusion. I found the most helpful thing a person did was to listen without judgment or injecting their personal perspective when I talked about the loss of my father.

Know that it's all right if the child talks about the loved one in the present tense, has dreams or nightmares, appears at times to feel nothing, is afraid to be left alone, is worried about health issues, cries often, wets the bed or loses appetite, idealizes the loved one, has headaches and stomach aches, withdraws, or acts out. As an adult when I heard the term *complicated grief* used to mourn the loss of a loved one to suicide I felt it accurately described my grieving process for my father. At first all my feelings were jumbled together, I had a hard time sorting them, and often didn't know what or how I was feeling. As one counselor told me, my unconscious did keep a list of all the feelings I had to face, and with time I was able to decipher each emotion and slowly progress through my grief process.

The most important thing you can provide an adolescent is unconditional love and support. Often times the closest people to the adolescent are also going through the grieving process of losing a loved one to suicide and cannot offer all the emotional support needed. Assigning a close friend of the family as a mentor for the child to aid with the grieving process and day-to-day needs such as driving to school, practices, counselors, and so forth, can be a tremendous help and make a difference in the child's life.

Look to the resources in the back of this book for more information on suicide and grief support.

Understanding Suicide

Why Did They Do It?

Attempting to decipher precisely the thoughts of the suicide victim is much like trying to understand a foreign language by eavesdropping on a conversation. You can analyze the sounds and syllables all day long, but it's not likely you're going to understand much of what was said.

—Jeffrey Jackson, American Association of Suicidology,
Handbook for Suicide Survivors

The question that occupies anyone impacted by a suicide death for some time is "why?" This inquiry has never completely left my mind regarding my father. Over the years I've struggled for answers by linking his suicide to his separation, our financial problems, or the death of his father a few years before.

The fact is there are several behavioral, environmental, and cultural risk factors that can lead to suicidal thoughts. Based on the accounts of those who have attempted suicide and lived to tell about it, the primary goal of a suicide is not to end life, but to end pain. My father was not in his right mind the day he chose to end his life. As for *why*—I believe I will never truly know. All I can do is go on living and try to focus on the memories of his life and not his death.

Following are a list of behavioral, cultural, and environmental risk factors that can lead to suicidal thoughts.

Behavioral Risk Factors

- Mental disorders, particularly mood disorders, schizophrenia, anxiety disorders, and certain personality disorders
- Alcohol and other substance use disorders
- Hopelessness
- Impulsive and/or aggressive tendencies
- History of trauma or abuse
- Some major physical illnesses
- Family history of suicide
- Talking directly or indirectly about dying or committing suicide
- Changes in sleeping habits (too much, too little)
- Changes in eating habits (sudden weight gain, weight loss)
- Discouragement about the future, self-criticism
- Recent lack of concern about physical appearance, hygiene
- Withdrawal from social contacts or communication difficulty
- Giving away prized possessions
- Drop in school grades or work performance
- Acquiring the means for suicide (guns, drugs, rope)
- Making final arrangements, writing a will
- Taking unusual risks
- Preoccupation with death through poetry and/or artwork
- Previous suicide attempts (80% of those who kill themselves have attempted it before)

Environmental Risk Factors

- Job or financial loss
- Easy access to lethal means
- Local clusters of suicide that have a contagious influence
- End of a serious relationship or divorce
- Loss of a loved one to suicide
- Death of a loved one
- Moving to a new location

Cultural Risk Factors

- Lack of social support and sense of isolation
- Stigma associated with help-seeking behavior
- Barriers to accessing health care, especially mental health and substance abuse treatment
- Certain cultural and religious beliefs (for instance, the belief that suicide is a noble resolution of a personal dilemma)

If you observe any of these risk factors, please seek help as soon as possible by contacting a mental health professional or calling 1-800-SUICIDE or 1-800-273-TALK for a referral.

Facts and Statistics

Suicide Information

The World Health Organization estimates that each year approximately one million people die from suicide. This is a global mortality rate of 16 per 100,000 or one death every 40 seconds.

The WHO further reports that in the last 45 years suicide rates have increased by 60% worldwide. Suicide is now among the three leading causes of death among those aged 15 to 44 (both sexes). Suicide attempts are up to 20 times more frequent than completed suicides.

Although suicide rates have traditionally been highest among elderly males, rates among young people have been increasing to such an extent that they are now the group at highest risk in a third of all countries.

Mental disorders (particularly depression and substance abuse) are associated with more than 90% of all cases of suicide. However, suicide results from many complex sociocultural factors, and is more likely to occur during periods of socioeconomic, family, and individual crisis (e.g., loss of a loved one, employment, or honor).

In the United States, the Centers for Disease Control reports that more people die from suicide than from homicide. In 1997, there were 1.5 times as many suicides as homicides. Overall, suicide is the eighth leading cause of death for all Americans, and is the third leading cause of death for young people aged 15 to 24. Males are four times more likely to die from suicide than are females. However, females are more likely to attempt suicide than are males.

Statistics about suicide are difficult to collate, and may be inaccurate because of the sensitivity of the issue, particularly in countries where suicide is an absolute taboo. You can find these and other suicide statistics in the following English language sites:

- Australia Statistics: Living Is for Everyone (http://www. livingisforeveryone.com.au): Australian suicide statistics.
- Canada Statistics: Canada Statistics Agency (http:// www40.statcan.ca): Canadian suicide statistics.
- International Statistics: World Health Organization (http://www.who.int): international suicide statistics, including the most recent global stats by country.
- New Zealand Statistics: New Zealand Health Information Service (http://www.nzhis.govt.nz): NZ suicide statistics.
- United Kingdom Statistics: U.K. Samaritans (http:// www.samaritans.org): suicide statistics for the United Kingdom and the Republic of Ireland.
- United States Statistics: American Association of Suicidology (http://www.suicidology.org): U.S. suicide statistics.

Other Resources

United States
Associations and Resources

American Association of Suicidology
5221 Wisconsin Avenue, NW
Washington, DC 20015
(202) 237-2280
www.suicidology.org

American Foundation for Suicide Prevention
120 Wall Street, 22nd Floor
New York, NY 10005
(212) 363-3500
www.afsp.org

Baton Rouge Crisis Intervention Center
4837 Revere Avenue
Baton Rouge, LA 70808
(225) 924-1431
www.brcic.org

Colorado Department of Public Health and
Environment
Office of Suicide Prevention
4300 Cherry Creek Drive South
Denver, CO 80246-1530
(303) 692-2539
www.cdphe.state.co.us/pp/suicide/index.html

The Compassionate Friends, Inc.
P. O. Box 3696
Oak Brook, IL 60522-3696
877-969-0010
www.compassionatefriends.org

Friends for Survival, Inc.
P.O. Box 214463
Sacramento, CA 95821
(800) 646-7322
www.friendsforsurvival.org

HEARTBEAT
2015 Devon
Colorado Springs, CO 80909
(719) 596-2575
www.heartbeatsurvivorsaftersuicide.org

Hope for Bereaved, Inc.
4500 Onondaga Blvd.
Syracuse, New York 13219
(315) 475-9675
www.hopeforbereaved.com

National Alliance on Mental Illness (NAMI)
Colonial Place Three
2107 Wilson Blvd., Suite 300
Arlington, VA 22201-3042
(888) 999-NAMI
www.nami.org

National Resource Center: Suicide Prevention and
Aftercare
www.thelink.org

Prevent Suicide Now
1-800-SUICIDE
1-800-273-TALK
www.preventsuicidenow.com

The Samaritans
P.O. Box 5228
Albany, NY 12205
518-689-0080
www.befrienders.org

SA/VE (Suicide Awareness/Voices of Education)
P.O. Box 24507
Minneapolis, MN 55424
(612) 946-7998
www.save.org

Sibling Survivors
www.siblingsurvivors.com

Suicide and Mental Health Association
International
P.O. Box 702
Sioux Falls, SD 57101-0702
www.suicideandmentalhealthassociation
international.org

Suicide Prevention Action Network USA (SPAN USA)
1025 Vermont Ave., NW, Suite 1066
Washington, DC 20005
(202) 449-3600
www.spanusa.org

Suicide Prevention Coalition of Colorado (SPCC)
http://suicideprevention-colorado.org/

Suicide Prevention Resource Center
Education Development Center, Inc.
1000 Potomac Street NW, Suite 350
Washington, DC 20007
877-GET-SPRC
www.sprc.org

Surviving Suicide
www.survivingsuicide.com

Yellow Ribbon Suicide Prevention Program
www.yellowribbon.org

International Associations and Resources

Canadian Association of Suicide Prevention (CASP)
www.suicideprevention.ca

Child Helpline International
www.childhelplineinternational.org

International Association for Suicide Prevention (IASP)
www.med.uio.no/iasp/

International Federation of Telephone Emergency Services (IFOTES)
www.ifotes.org

Life Line International
www.lifeline.web.za

Suicide Information and Education Center
Centre for Suicide Prevention
www.suicideinfo.ca

Telephone Helplines Association (United Kingdom)
www.helplines.org.uk

Acknowledgments

Writing this book was another step in my journey of healing as a survivor of suicide. I'm immensely grateful to my husband, Wright, for his encouragement to tell my story. I also want to thank my children for their patience during the many evenings and weekends I was typing away on the computer. I love you!

Thank you to my mother and sisters for understanding my need to share our experience with the world and for allowing me to make public such a private and painful event.

I'm so appreciative to the wonderful friends and colleagues who helped mold this book. Melanie Mulhall, my editor and mentor, thank you for your talented writing and creative contributions. Dr. Lee Jampolsky, I appreciate your invaluable counsel, which helped me face my fears to produce a better product.

Finally, thank you Jerome and Gail Potts, Elizabeth Hugus, Wright Hugus Jr., Christin O'Neill, Stephanie Racz, LaRita Archibald, Karen Storsteen, Tamra Monahan, Nicole Heintz, and Connie Savander for your emotional support and input during this project.

About the Author

A former marketing and communications executive, Carrie Stark Hugus is married and the mother of two children. She is a Colorado native, and lives with her family and dog, in Highlands Ranch.

Visit the author's Web site at www.affirmpublications.com.